THE BATTLE OF
ANTIETAM

"The Bloodiest Day of Battle"

By **Larry Hama** Illustrated by **Scott Moore**

rosen publishing's
**rosen
central**

New York

Published in 2007 by The Rosen Publishing Group, Inc.
29 East 21st Street, New York, NY 10010

First edition, 2007

Photo credits: Pg. 4 Library of Congress; pg. 5 (top) Courtesy of Chrysalis Picture Library, (bottom) U.S. Navy; pg. 7 Library of Congress; pg. 44 Library of Congress; pg. 45 Library of Congress

Simone Drinkwater, Series Editor/Osprey Publishing
Nel Yomtov, Series Editor/Rosen Book Works
Geeta Sobha, Editor/Rosen Book Works

Library of Congress Cataloging-in-Publication Data

Hama, Larry.
    The Battle of Antietam: "the bloodiest day of battle"/by Larry Hama.—1st ed.
    p. cm.—(Graphic battles of the Civil War)
    Includes bibliographical references and index.
    ISBN-13   978-1-4042-0775-2 (lib.)   978-1-4042-6475-5 (pbk.)
    ISBN-10   1-4042-0775-9 (lib.)   1-4042-6475-2 (pbk.)
    6-pack ISBN-13   978-1-4042-6270-6   6-pack ISBN-10   1-4042-6270-9
    1. Antietam, Battle of, Md., 1862—Juvenile literature. I. Title. II. Series.

E474.65.H36 2007
973.7'336—dc22

                  2006007186

CONTENTS

THE AMERICAN CIVIL WAR, 1861-1865

By the 1850s, there were many economic and political differences between the Northern and Southern states in America. The biggest difference was over the issue of slavery. The South's economy depended upon slaves to work the plantations that grew crops such as tobacco and cotton. In the North, slavery was illegal.

When Abraham Lincoln, an antislavery candidate, was elected president in 1860, the South believed that their way of life would be destroyed. Soon after, South Carolina seceded, or left, the Union. More Southern states followed. They formed the Confederate States of America, a separate government.

Anger built between the two sides. Finally, on April 12, 1861, Southern forces bombed Fort Sumter in South Carolina. Over the next four years, many bloody battles were fought, but none more terrible than the Battle of Antietam on September 17, 1862. On that day, more than 23,000 American soldiers were killed or wounded—more than on any other day in U.S. history.

KEY COMMANDERS

GEORGE McCLELLAN
Major general and general in chief of the Union armies. President Lincoln removed McClellan from command after the Battle of Antietam.

ROBERT E. LEE
Commander of the Army of Northern Virginia. Outnumbered at Antietam, Lee's army withstood powerful Union attacks, but he was forced to withdraw to Virginia.

AMBROSE BURNSIDE
Commander of two corps at Antietam, he was appointed McClellan's successor. In December 1862, Joseph Hooker replaced Burnside.

JOHN GORDON
Confederate general Gordon's unit defended a key position on the sunken road at Antietam. Gordon also commanded forces at Gettysburg, Chancellorsville, and the Wilderness.

By September 1862, the American Civil War was in its seventeenth month. Any hope that it would be a short war was gone. The South had successfully fought a defensive war. The Union showed no sign of giving up and accepting the Confederacy as a separate country.

Each side had advantages. The population of the North was nearly four times larger than that of the South, excluding slaves. Most of the food-growing land and manufacturers were in the North. The South grew plantation crops, such as cotton and tobacco. The South's best chance was to fight until either the North gave up or European nations stepped in to help them.

In June 1862, Lincoln showed his cabinet a proclamation that would free all of the slaves in Southern states on January 1, 1863. His cabinet was shocked. The Union had suffered many defeats, and they thought the proclamation would seem to be only an attempt to create a slave revolt to

★ The South's economy was based on agriculture. Crops such as tobacco and cotton were grown on plantations that were worked by black slaves.

cover the North's failures. To carry out his plans, Lincoln needed a military victory quickly.

At this time, the Confederacy was making plans to invade the North. General Robert E. Lee was in command of the Southern army. On September 4, 1862, Lee's Army of Northern Virginia crossed the Potomac River into Maryland. Lee began to move on the Union garrison at the important railroad center at Harper's Ferry, Virginia. In command of the Union's Army of the Potomac was General George McClellan. McClellan cautiously pushed his forces west toward Lee and the Blue Ridge Mountain passes.

On September 13, McClellan got a lucky break. Union soldiers found a piece of paper, wrapped around three cigars. It was a Confederate note describing the positions of all of Lee's forces and their movement orders. Lee had split his army into five parts. McClellan was closer to each part than they were to each other. If McClellan

★ Harper's Ferry was an important railroad center in Virginia. It was occupied by the Union army until Confederate general Robert E. Lee's forces took control of it in September 1862.

moved quickly, he could smash each part, and the war would be over.

However, McClellan thought he was outnumbered, and he moved slowly. His troops captured the mountain passes the following day. Lee knew that his orders had been discovered, but he also knew that McClellan was cautious. Lee captured Harper's Ferry and its 10,000-man force five miles away. Then he brought together most of his scattered army and moved north to Sharpsburg, Virginia.

★ Ships like the USS Vanderbilt blocked all Southern ports to stop the Confederates from sending supplies to their armies.

In Sharpsburg, Lee's men were in an area that was mostly farmland with wooded areas scattered about. The Southern forces had their backs to the Potomac River. Antietam Creek was to their front. Lee was still missing part of his army, the Light Division under General A. P. Hill.

The Union army was 87,000 strong. It was divided into six infantry corps

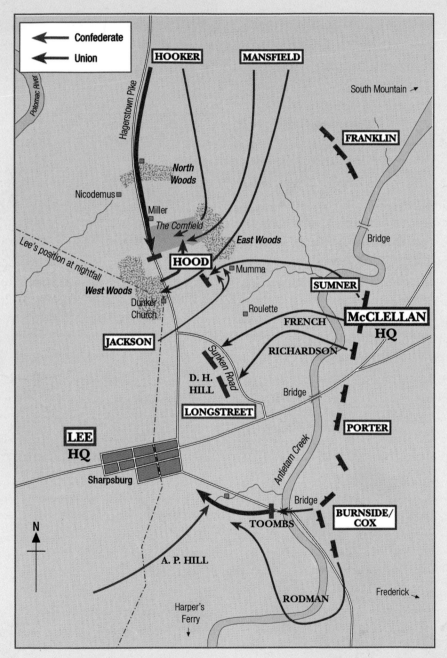

★ At the Battle of Antietam, fought on September 17, 1862, the Union army far outnumbered the Confederates. Despite this, the Confederates were able to defend against several Union attacks before retreating to Virginia. Antietam was the first major battle of the Civil War to take place on Northern soil.

and a separate cavalry command. Lee's army, 40,000 strong, was made up of smaller units, divisions, and brigades, under Generals Thomas "Stonewall" Jackson and James Longstreet.

McClellan's main attack would be at the northern end of Lee's line, against Jackson. Four infantry corps would attack, two from the north and two from the east. Meanwhile, at the southern end, General Ambrose Burnside would make a diversionary attack with his corps. In the center, McClellan's infantry corps would support both flanks for an attack straight across the creek.

The Union attack began at dawn, September 17. General "Fighting Joe" Hooker advanced down the Hagerstown Pike toward Dunker Church. Hooker's men fought through the North Woods into a cornfield. They were counter-attacked by Confederate John Bell Hood's Texas Brigade and were thrown back. The cornfield would change hands over a dozen times that day.

Then, Union general Joseph Mansfield attacked across the same ground, this time through the East Woods and the same cornfield. His men briefly captured the church, only to lose it to another counterattack.

At 9:00 A.M., the Union II Corps joined the attack. Part of the corps, under commander General Edwin "Bull" Sumner, turned toward the church. They were hit by Jackson's last reserves in the West Woods. A horrified Sumner told General Franklin not to attack with his corps. McClellan agreed. Yet unknown to them, Jackson was beaten. He had run out of troops and ammunition.

Meanwhile, the remainder of Sumner's corps veered toward the center of the battlefield. There, Confederate troops, dug in along a sunken country road, shot them down in rows as they advanced.

By 1:00 P.M., two Union regiments had fought their way into the battle-field's center. Union soldiers took deadly aim, left and right. Hundreds of Confederates were killed. They were almost the last of Lee's troops.

★ **Gen. Robert E. Lee**

★ *Confederate general Robert E. Lee was in charge of the Confederate army for the entire war.*

Burnside, meanwhile, had begun his own attack at 10:00 A.M. He sent his troops across a narrow stone bridge. By 1:00 P.M., Burnside had captured the bridge. In the afternoon, Burnside advanced against the last remains of Confederate resistance. Then, at 4:00 P.M., A. P. Hill's Light Division finally reached the battle-field. Hill hit Burnside's left flank and drove him back to the bridge. At that point, the battle ended. Neither side wished to continue the bloodiest day of battle ever fought on American soil.

THE BATTLE OF ANTIETAM:
"The Bloodiest Day of Battle"

IN SEPTEMBER 1862, CONFEDERATE TROOPS FLED THE TOWN OF FREDERICK, MARYLAND, AS THE UNION ARMY APPROACHED.

ONE STORY TELLS OF BARBARA FRIETCHIE PROUDLY WAVING A UNION FLAG AT UNION SOLDIERS.

THE STORY GREW TO BECOME FRIETCHIE WAVING THE FLAG DEFIANTLY AT CONFEDERATE GENERAL STONEWALL JACKSON.

JOHN GREENLEAF WHITTIER WROTE THE POEM "BARBARA FRIETCHIE."

THE REAL STORY IS NOT NEARLY AS UPLIFTING - AND A LOT BLOODIER.

AMERICAN CHILDREN WOULD LEARN ABOUT THE BATTLE OF ANTIETAM FROM THIS POEM. HOWEVER, THERE WAS VERY LITTLE TRUTH IN IT.

ON SEPTEMBER 12, 1862, UNION TROOPS ENTERED FREDERICK. THEY CAMPED ON THE SAME GROUNDS THAT THE CONFEDERATES HAD USED.

THE NEXT MORNING, CORPORAL MITCHELL AND A SERGEANT FROM THE 27TH INDIANA FOUND THREE CIGARS WRAPPED IN A SHEET OF PAPER.

THIS MUST BE OUR LUCKY DAY!

WHAT'S ALL THAT WRITING ON THE PAPER?

IT SAYS, "BY COMMAND OF GENERAL R. E. LEE!"

THIS HAS TO GO TO HEADQUARTERS RIGHT AWAY!

SPECIAL ORDER 191

SHORTLY, AT GENERAL McCLELLAN'S HEADQUARTERS . . .

SIR, THESE ORDERS SAY EXACTLY WHERE THE CONFEDERATE ARMY IS LOCATED, WHERE IT'S GOING, AND HOW IT'S GOING TO GET THERE.

COULD THIS BE A TRICK? IF I ATTACK, I MIGHT BE LEADING THE ARMY INTO A TRAP.

GENERAL McCLELLAN, YOU CAN CATCH THE ENTIRE ARMY OF NORTHERN VIRGINIA UNAWARE AND END THE WAR!

OR LOSE THE ENTIRE ARMY OF THE POTOMAC IF THE ENEMY OUTNUMBERS US.

AT THE BATTLE OF SOUTH MOUNTAIN, FOUGHT ON SEPTEMBER 14, McCLELLAN ATTACKED CAUTIOUSLY. HE SENT PART OF HIS ARMY WESTWARD THROUGH A MOUNTAIN GAP TO ENGAGE LEE.

HIS PLAN WAS TO "CUT THE ENEMY IN TWO AND BEAT HIM IN DETAIL."

THE PLAN MIGHT HAVE WORKED HAD HE USED ALL THE TROOPS HE HAD AVAILABLE.

THE NORTHERN ARMY NEEDED A VICTORY.

HOWEVER, ROBERT E. LEE WAS ABLE TO GET AWAY WITH HIS ARMY INTACT.

WE LIVE TO FIGHT ANOTHER DAY!

PERHAPS LEE FELT THAT HE COULD NOT RETURN TO VIRGINIA WITHOUT A CLEAR-CUT VICTORY, SO HE DECIDED TO STAND AND FIGHT.

LEE REGROUPED HIS FORCES AND SET UP DEFENSIVE POSITIONS AROUND THE TOWN OF SHARPSBURG, ABOUT 30 MILES NORTHWEST OF FREDERICK.

MCCLELLAN TOOK HIS TIME PURSUING LEE. FINALLY, ON SEPTEMBER 17, HE BEGAN HIS ASSAULT ON THE CONFEDERATES.

MAJOR GENERAL JOSEPH HOOKER WAS GIVEN THE TASK OF MAKING THE INITIAL ATTACK AT THE CONFEDERATE LEFT . . .

JACKSON

. . . WHERE STONEWALL JACKSON WAS IN COMMAND.

AT 6:15 A.M., HOOKER'S TROOPS CAME OUT OF THE NORTH WOODS AFTER A NIGHT OF SKIRMISHING BETWEEN PICKETS ON BOTH SIDES.

THEY WERE FACING A 40-ACRE FIELD OF CORN. FROM THAT DAY ON, IT WOULD BE KNOWN SIMPLY AS "THE CORNFIELD."

GENERAL HOOKER SAW CONFEDERATE BAYONETS GLEAMING ABOVE THE TALL CORN. HE KNEW "THE FIELD WAS FILLED WITH THE ENEMY."

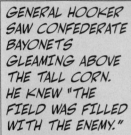

FEDERAL ARTILLERY FIRED A WITHERING BARRAGE INTO THE CORNFIELD TO PREPARE THE WAY.

LATER, HOOKER WROTE THAT " . . . EVERY STALK . . . WAS CUT AS CLOSELY AS COULD HAVE BEEN DONE WITH A KNIFE."

WHEN THE ROAR OF THE ARTILLERY DIED DOWN, THE UNION INFANTRY ADVANCED INTO THE CORNFIELD.

OH, MY...

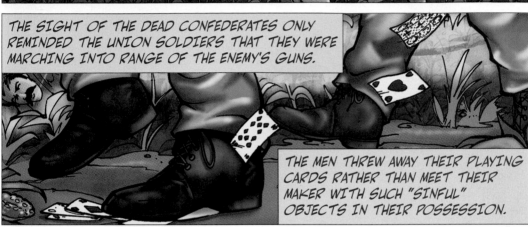

THE SIGHT OF THE DEAD CONFEDERATES ONLY REMINDED THE UNION SOLDIERS THAT THEY WERE MARCHING INTO RANGE OF THE ENEMY'S GUNS.

THE MEN THREW AWAY THEIR PLAYING CARDS RATHER THAN MEET THEIR MAKER WITH SUCH "SINFUL" OBJECTS IN THEIR POSSESSION.

SOME OF THE FIRST ENCOUNTERS TOOK PLACE AT A RANGE OF 30 YARDS OR LESS.

FIRE AT WILL!

MEN STOOD THEIR GROUND AND FIRED. THEN THEY RELOADED AND FIRED AGAIN, AND AGAIN, AND AGAIN.

THIS WAS NOT A SIMPLE TASK BY ANY MEANS, ESPECIALLY IN THE HEAT OF BATTLE.

BOTH ARMIES WERE ARMED WITH RIFLE MUSKETS.

. . . WHICH WAS A PAPER CYLINDER THAT HELD THE LEAD BULLET AND GUNPOWDER.

HE HAD TO RIP THE CARTRIDGE WITH HIS TEETH.

THE RIFLE WAS HELD MUZZLE UP. THE SOLDIER REACHED INTO A CASE ON HIS BELT AND TOOK OUT A CARTRIDGE . . .

NEXT, HE POURED THE GUNPOWDER DOWN THE BARREL AND STUFFED THE BULLET INTO THE MUZZLE.

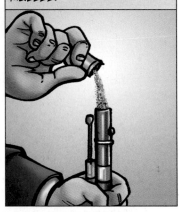

HE USED THE RAMROD TO JAM BULLET, PAPER, AND GUNPOWDER DOWN THE BARREL.

THE RAMROD WAS THEN REPLACED USING JUST THE LITTLE FINGER.

THE HAMMER WAS DRAWN TO HALF COCK AND A PERCUSSION CAP WAS PLACED ON THE NIPPLE.

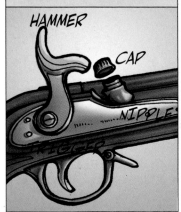

HAMMER

CAP

NIPPLE

THE RIFLE WAS SHOULDERED, BROUGHT TO FULL COCK, AIMED . . .

. . . AND FIRED.

14

UNION MAJOR GENERAL GEORGE MEADE LED A DIVISION OF PENNSYLVANIANS AT THE CENTER OF THE ATTACK.

MEADE

A GEORGIA REGIMENT ROSE OUT OF THE CORN 30 FEET AWAY. THEY KNOCKED OUT HALF A REGIMENT OF PENNSYLVANIANS IN ONE VOLLEY.

THE UNION SOLDIERS BEGAN TO RETREAT, BUT A YOUNG PRIVATE STOPPED THEM.

ARE YOU GOING TO RUN LIKE DOGS, OR DIE LIKE MEN?!

THE MEN RALLIED TO HIM, THE LINE WAS RE-FORMED . . .

. . . AND HELD.

THEN THEY ADVANCED.

MEANWHILE, McCLELLAN AND HIS STAFF WERE OBSERVING THE BATTLE FROM THEIR HILLTOP HEADQUARTERS.

THE CORNFIELD IS AS GOOD AS TAKEN, SIR.

I WANT THAT FIELD SECURED ALL THE WAY SOUTH TO THAT LITTLE WHITE HOUSE.*

* A CHURCH OF THE DUNKER SECT

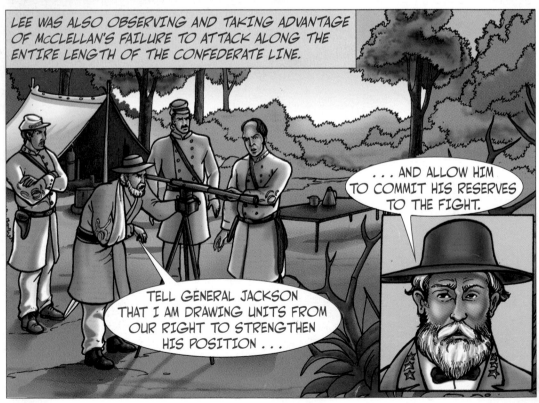

LEE WAS ALSO OBSERVING AND TAKING ADVANTAGE OF McCLELLAN'S FAILURE TO ATTACK ALONG THE ENTIRE LENGTH OF THE CONFEDERATE LINE.

. . . AND ALLOW HIM TO COMMIT HIS RESERVES TO THE FIGHT.

TELL GENERAL JACKSON THAT I AM DRAWING UNITS FROM OUR RIGHT TO STRENGTHEN HIS POSITION . . .

THOSE RESERVES WERE THE TEXAS BRIGADE. THEY WERE COMMANDED BY BRIGADIER GENERAL JOHN BELL HOOD.

THE TEXANS CHARGED INTO THE FIELD AND WERE MET BY BLASTS OF SHOTGUN-LIKE CANISTERS FIRED BY UNION ARTILLERY.

OVER AND OVER, THE TEXAS LONE STAR FLAG WAS SHOT DOWN.

OVER AND OVER, THE FLAG WAS TAKEN BACK UP TO LEAD THE WAY.

AS THE TEXANS CHARGED, THE UNION TROOPS FELL BACK, GIVING UP THEIR HARD-EARNED GROUND.

IT SEEMED THAT THE TEXANS COULD NOT BE STOPPED.

A COLONEL OF THE 17TH GEORGIA SAID, "NOT ONE SHOWED ANY DISPOSITION, NOTWITHSTANDING THEIR TERRIBLE LOSS, TO FALL BACK OR FLINCH FROM THE ENEMY."

THE TEXAS BRIGADE FOUGHT ALL THE WAY ACROSS THE 40-ACRE CORNFIELD BEFORE THEY WERE TURNED BACK.

GENERAL HOOKER WROTE IN HIS REPORT, "IT WAS NEVER MY FORTUNE TO WITNESS A MORE BLOODY, DISMAL BATTLEFIELD."

THE TEXAS BRIGADE'S LOSSES WERE STAGGERING. ENTIRE COMPANIES HAD BEEN WIPED OUT.

GENERAL HOOD, WHERE ARE YOUR MEN?

GENERAL LEE, I REGRET TO INFORM YOU, THEY ARE LYING ON THE FIELD.

MEANWHILE, UNION MAJOR GENERAL JOSEPH K. F. MANSFIELD LED HIS TWO DIVISIONS THROUGH THE EAST WOODS TO THE FIGHT.

MANSFIELD NEVER MADE IT TO THE CORNFIELD. HE WAS SHOT THROUGH THE STOMACH AND TAKEN TO THE REAR, WHERE HE DIED.

HIS LAST ORDERS WERE INSTRUCTIONS TO LOOK AFTER HIS HORSE.

ONE OF THE UNITS UNDER MANSFIELD'S COMMAND WAS THE 27TH INDIANA.

THE INDIANA BOYS STOOD THEIR GROUND IN THE MIDDLE OF THE CORNFIELD.

GO GET 'EM, BOYS!

EACH MAN USED UP ALL HIS AMMUNITION, 100 ROUNDS PER MAN, THEN SEARCHED THE DEAD AND WOUNDED FOR MORE.

SORRY, BILLY . . .

THEY FIRED THEIR MUSKETS FOR SO LONG THAT THE GUNS BECAME TOO HOT TO HANDLE.

EEEE-YOW!

ONE OF THE WOUNDED WAS CORPORAL MITCHELL, WHO HAD FOUND THE LOST ORDER WRAPPED AROUND THE CIGARS.

HAD TO TURN THOSE DARN ORDERS IN, DIDN'T YOU?

POSSESSION OF THE CORNFIELD WENT BACK AND FORTH ALL MORNING.

THE CONFEDERATES MADE ONE LAST CHARGE. THEY HOPED TO CARRY ALL THE WAY ACROSS TO THE NORTH WOODS.

BUT THEY WERE CAUGHT BETWEEN A MURDEROUS VOLLEY OF RIFLE FIRE FROM THE EAST WOODS . . .

. . . AND A BARRAGE OF ARTILLERY FROM THE SLOPE NORTH OF THE CORNFIELD.

BARELY FOUR HOURS AFTER THE FIRST SHOT WAS FIRED, CLOSE TO 12,000 MEN LAY DEAD OR WOUNDED IN THE CORNFIELD AS WELL AS THE NEARBY WOODS AND FARMYARDS.

AROUND NOON, CLARA BARTON, A FORMER CLERK FOR THE U.S. PATENT OFFICE, ARRIVED AT THE NORTH END OF THE CORNFIELD WITH A WAGON FULL OF BANDAGES.

UNTIL HER ARRIVAL, THE SURGEONS HAD BEEN DRESSING WOUNDS WITH CORN HUSKS.

BARTON STAYED TO COMFORT AND TEND TO THE WOUNDED.

TH-THANK YOU, MA'AM.

A STRAY BULLET KILLED A MAN AS SHE GAVE HIM A DRINK OF WATER.

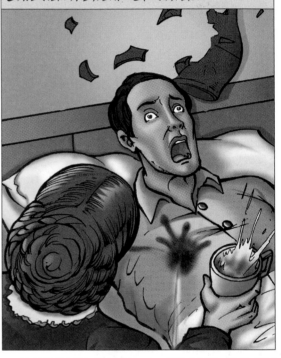

THE BULLET HAD PASSED THROUGH BARTON'S SLEEVE BEFORE HITTING THE MAN.

BRAVELY, CLARA BARTON CONTINUED HER WORK THROUGH THE LONG NIGHT.

SHE WOULD LATER GO ON TO FOUND THE AMERICAN RED CROSS IN 1881.

SOUTH OF THE DUNKER CHURCH WAS A COUNTRY ROAD THAT ZIGZAGGED SOUTHWEST FOR LESS THAN A MILE.

EROSION AND HARD USE HAD WORN THE ROAD DOWN.

THIS SUNKEN ROAD BECAME THE CENTER OF LEE'S DEFENSIVE LINE.

THE TROOPS IN THE SUNKEN ROAD WERE TOTALLY PROTECTED.

ATTACKERS WOULD BE COMPLETELY IN THE OPEN.

TWO DIVISIONS OF UNION TROOPS UNDER GENERALS FRENCH AND RICHARDSON WERE ABOUT TO ASSAULT THE SUNKEN ROAD AS THE BATTLE RAGED IN THE CORNFIELD.

... UNION GENERALS FRENCH AND RICHARDSON SHOULD HAVE BEEN NORTH, SUPPORTING GENERAL SUMNER AS HE SOUGHT TO REGAIN CONTROL OF THE CORNFIELD.

THERE HAD BEEN CONFUSION AT HIGHER LEVELS OF COMMAND . . .

THOUSANDS OF MEN WOULD PAY IN BLOOD FOR THE ERROR.

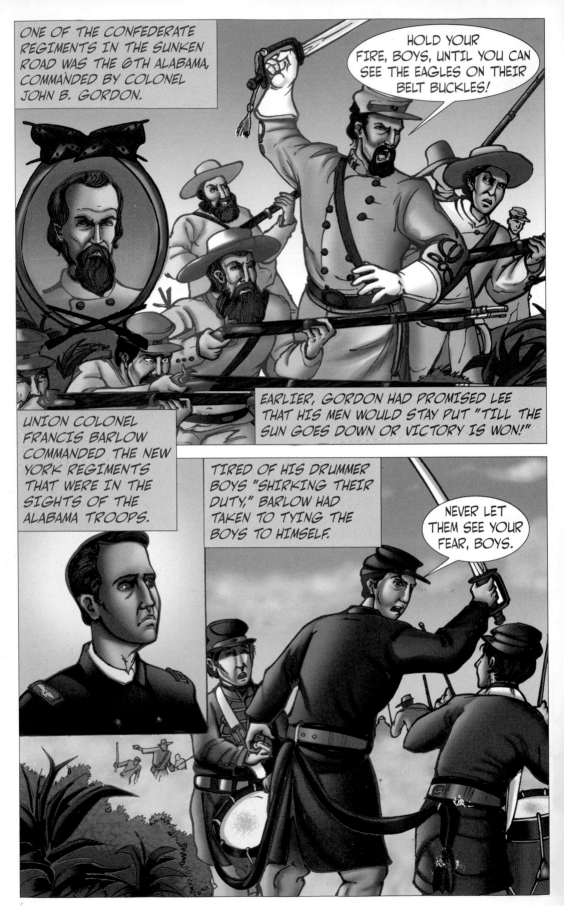

ONE OF THE CONFEDERATE REGIMENTS IN THE SUNKEN ROAD WAS THE 6TH ALABAMA, COMMANDED BY COLONEL JOHN B. GORDON.

HOLD YOUR FIRE, BOYS, UNTIL YOU CAN SEE THE EAGLES ON THEIR BELT BUCKLES!

EARLIER, GORDON HAD PROMISED LEE THAT HIS MEN WOULD STAY PUT "TILL THE SUN GOES DOWN OR VICTORY IS WON!"

UNION COLONEL FRANCIS BARLOW COMMANDED THE NEW YORK REGIMENTS THAT WERE IN THE SIGHTS OF THE ALABAMA TROOPS.

TIRED OF HIS DRUMMER BOYS "SHIRKING THEIR DUTY," BARLOW HAD TAKEN TO TYING THE BOYS TO HIMSELF.

NEVER LET THEM SEE YOUR FEAR, BOYS.

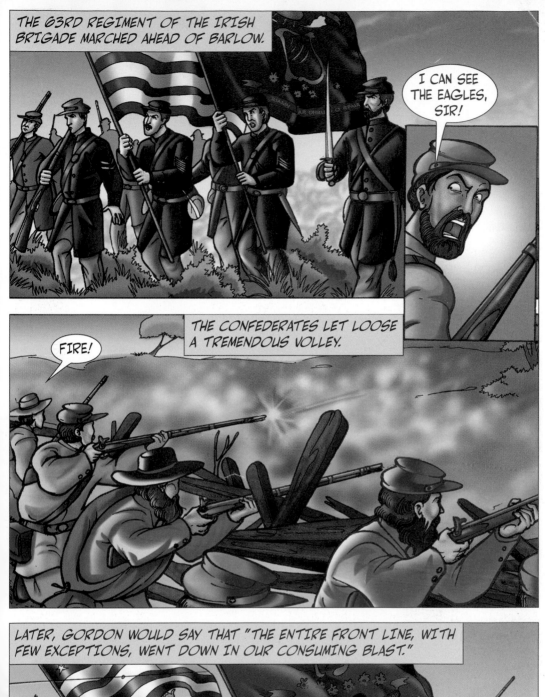

THE 63RD REGIMENT OF THE IRISH BRIGADE MARCHED AHEAD OF BARLOW.

I CAN SEE THE EAGLES, SIR!

FIRE!

THE CONFEDERATES LET LOOSE A TREMENDOUS VOLLEY.

LATER, GORDON WOULD SAY THAT "THE ENTIRE FRONT LINE, WITH FEW EXCEPTIONS, WENT DOWN IN OUR CONSUMING BLAST."

THE IRISH BRIGADE GAVE
AS GOOD AS THEY TOOK.

BARLOW SAID THAT THEY WERE
"BRISKLY ENGAGING THE ENEMY."

PROTECTED AS THEY WERE, THE ALABAMA REGIMENT
WAS STILL TAKING FEARFUL LOSSES.

COLONEL GORDON WAS SHOT
THROUGH HIS RIGHT CALF. THE
OFFICER HE WAS SPEAKING TO WAS
NOT SO LUCKY.

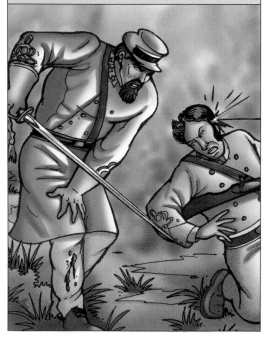

MEN WERE SHOOTING AT EACH OTHER
AT SUCH CLOSE RANGE THAT THEY
WERE NOT MISSING MANY SHOTS.

GORDON WAS SHOT
AGAIN, IN THE SAME LEG.

COLONEL BARLOW HAD MOVED HIS REGIMENTS TO A POSITION WHERE THEY COULD FIRE DOWN THE LENGTH OF THE CONFEDERATE LINE.

THIS IS AS GOOD A SPOT AS ANY!

LET 'EM HAVE IT, BOYS!

WE WERE SHOOTING THEM LIKE SHEEP IN A PEN.

SO SAID SERGEANT CHARLES FULLER OF THE 61ST NEW YORK.

COLONEL GORDON WAS SHOT A THIRD TIME, THROUGH HIS LEFT ARM.

SIR, YOU MUST GO TO THE REAR AND HAVE YOUR WOUNDS TAKEN CARE OF!

ON OUR HONOR, WE SHALL STAY TO THE LAST!

I CANNOT CONSENT TO LEAVE YOU IN SUCH A CRISIS.

GORDON WAS SHOT A FOURTH TIME. THE SHOT FORCED A WAD OF CLOTHING INTO THE WOUND.

HERE, PRIVATE! TELL THE MEN AT THE END OF THE LINE THAT I AM STILL ON THE FIELD AND THAT I INTEND TO STAY HERE.

THE YOUNG PRIVATE WENT LESS THAN 50 YARDS WHEN HE WAS KILLED.

GORDON SET OUT TO TELL THE MEN HIMSELF . . .

...BUT WAS HIT IN THE FACE. THE BULLET PASSED THROUGH, BARELY MISSING AN IMPORTANT VEIN.

HE FELL UNCONSCIOUS WITH HIS FACE IN HIS CAP.

GORDON WOULD HAVE DROWNED IN HIS OWN BLOOD HAD IT NOT DRAINED OUT OF HIS CAP THROUGH A HOLE MADE PREVIOUSLY BY A NORTHERNER'S BULLET.*

*AMAZINGLY, GORDON WOULD SURVIVE HIS WOUNDS AND THE WAR.

COLONEL GORDON WAS TAKEN FROM THE FIELD. LIEUTENANT COLONEL LIGHTFOOT TOOK COMMAND.

IN HIS RUSH TO ORGANIZE HIS MEN TO RETURN FIRE AGAINST BARLOW, LIGHTFOOT GAVE THE WRONG ORDER.

RIGHT! ABOUT FACE! MARCH!

I MEANT, *FILES RIGHT! ABOUT! MARCH!*

BUT IT WAS TOO LATE. HIS TROOPS THOUGHT HE WAS ORDERING A RETREAT, AND THEY ABANDONED THEIR POSITIONS.

COLONEL BARLOW AND HIS NEW YORKERS SURGED INTO THE SUNKEN ROAD AND TOOK IT AFTER A DEVASTATING EXCHANGE OF FIRE.

BARLOW'S MEN STOOD UPON THE DEAD AND DYING, THREE DEEP IN THE BOTTOM OF THE ROAD, AS THEY SHOT AT THE RETREATING CONFEDERATES.

FROM THEN ON, THE SUNKEN ROAD WAS KNOWN AS "BLOODY LANE."

UNION LOSSES AT THE SUNKEN ROAD WERE ABOUT 3,000. THE CONFEDERATES LOST 2,600 MEN THERE . . .

. . . AND THEY HAD NO RESERVES LEFT AT ALL.

THE FEDERALS, ON THE OTHER HAND, HAD REGIMENTS TO SPARE.

TWENTY THOUSAND FRESH TROOPS WERE WAITING FOR ORDERS THAT NEVER CAME.

McCLELLAN STILL BELIEVED THAT HE WAS VASTLY OUTNUMBERED BY LEE.

SIR, GENERAL SUMNER CANNOT ATTACK AS ORDERED.

HIS COMMAND IS CUT UP AND DEMORALIZED!

SIR, GENERALS FRANKLIN AND HANCOCK ARE STANDING BY TO ATTACK! THEY SAY THEY CAN BEAT THE CONFEDERATES DECISIVELY!

IF THE ATTACK FAILS, THE DAY WILL BE LOST.

THE ATTACK WAS NOT ORDERED. ANOTHER OPPORTUNITY TO END THE WAR WAS LOST.

MCCLELLAN'S FAILURE TO ACT DECISIVELY SHOWED THE MAIN DIFFERENCE BETWEEN HIS VIEW OF WAR AND LEE'S.

MCCLELLAN PROBABLY SAW WAR AS A PERSONAL TEST OF HIS EGO. HE WAS VAIN, SELF-RIGHTEOUS, AND AMBITIOUS.

HE MAY HAVE THOUGHT OF HIS ARMY AS HE THOUGHT OF HIS HORSE. HE DID NOT WANT TO SEE IT HURT OR TREATED BADLY.

A LOST BATTLE HURT HIM DEEPLY AND PERSONALLY.

LEE BELIEVED THAT WAR WAS A DIVINE ACT.

... AND THAT THE SOUTH WOULD WIN BECAUSE IT HAD RIGHT ON ITS SIDE.

THIS ALLOWED LEE TO ACCEPT TERRIBLE CASUALTIES AND TAKE RISKS . . .

... WHILE MCCLELLAN COULD NOT.

IF THERE WERE THREE DISTINCT PHASES TO THE BATTLE OF ANTIETAM, THE CORNFIELD WAS THE FIRST, THE BLOODY LANE WAS THE SECOND . . .

. . . AND THE EVENTS AT A LITTLE STONE BRIDGE OVER THE ANTIETAM CREEK, ON THE FAR RIGHT OF LEE'S LINE, WERE TO BECOME THE THIRD.

McCLELLAN ORDERED UNION GENERAL AMBROSE BURNSIDE TO TAKE THE BRIDGE AT 8:00 A.M.

BURNSIDE

BURNSIDE HAD MORE THAN 12,500 TROOPS AT HIS DISPOSAL.

CONFEDERATE GENERAL ROBERT TOOMBS WAS HOLDING THE BRIDGE WITH ONLY 400 MEN . . .

COME ON, YANKEES!

. . . BUT THEY WERE DUG INTO HIDDEN PITS AND SNIPING FROM THE TREES.

UNION COLONEL GEORGE CROOK LED THREE REGIMENTS OF OHIO VOLUNTEERS AGAINST THE BRIDGE . . .

. . . OR HE WOULD HAVE, HAD THEY NOT GOTTEN LOST. DOZENS WERE SHOT THROUGH THE TREES.

UNION GENERAL S. D. STURGIS, COMMANDING THE 2ND MARYLAND AND THE 6TH HAMPSHIRE, MADE THE SECOND ASSAULT.

AT LEAST HE HAD THE ADVANTAGE OF KNOWING WHERE THE BRIDGE WAS . . .

. . . BUT THE KNOWLEDGE DID HIM LITTLE GOOD IN LIGHT OF CONFEDERATE SHARPSHOOTERS AND ARTILLERY.

THE TASK FELL TO THE 51ST NEW YORK AND THE 51ST PENNSYLVANIA UNDER THE COMMAND OF COLONEL EDWARD FERRERO.

GENERAL BURNSIDE REQUESTS THAT THE TWO 51ST REGIMENTS TAKE THAT BRIDGE. WILL YOU DO IT?

GIVE US OUR WHISKEY, AND WE'LL DO IT!

FERRERO AGREED TO DO JUST THAT. THE TWO 51ST REGIMENTS STORMED THE BRIDGE AND TOOK IT.

A FEW DAYS LATER, FERRERO WAS PROMOTED TO BRIGADIER GENERAL AND HAD TWO BARRELS OF WHISKEY SENT TO HIS TROOPS.

TOOMBS AND HIS GEORGIA MEN FELL BACK TOWARD SHARPSBURG. THEY WERE OUT OF AMMUNITION.

THEY HAD INFLICTED MORE THAN 500 CASUALTIES WHILE LOSING 160 OF THEIR OWN.

SOUTH OF SHARPSBURG, THE 9TH NEW YORK ZOUAVES* ADVANCED ON A STRONG CONFEDERATE POSITION BEHIND A STONE WALL ATOP A LOW RIDGE.

* ZOUAVES WERE AMERICAN REGIMENTS DRESSED LIKE ALGERIAN TROOPS OF THE OLD FRENCH ARMY.

WE CAN'T STAY HERE! WE'LL BE CHOPPED TO BITS!

WE MUST TAKE THE ARTILLERY! CHARGE!

LIEUTENANT COLONEL EDGAR KIMBALL LED THE CHARGE. THE CONFEDERATE GUNNERS FLED.

THE CONFEDERATES BEHIND THE WALL WERE MADE OF STERNER STUFF . . .

. . . BUT THEY BROKE AND RAN AS WELL.

ONE ZOUAVE LATER DESCRIBED HIS EXPERIENCE VERY VIVIDLY . . .

" . . . THE WHOLE LANDSCAPE TURNED RED."

OF THE 600 MEN OF THE 9TH NEW YORK WHO MADE THAT CHARGE, 220 FELL.

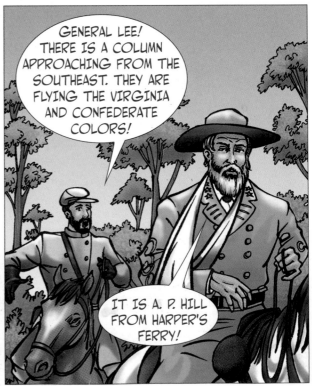

GENERAL LEE! THERE IS A COLUMN APPROACHING FROM THE SOUTHEAST. THEY ARE FLYING THE VIRGINIA AND CONFEDERATE COLORS!

IT IS A. P. HILL FROM HARPER'S FERRY!

HILL'S DIVISION HAD MARCHED 17 MILES IN 8 HOURS.

MAJOR GENERAL AMBROSE POWELL HILL HAD OFTEN BEEN BITTERLY AT ODDS WITH HIS SUPERIORS . . .

HILL

. . . BUT LEE HUGGED HILL WARMLY WHEN HE ARRIVED.

HILL'S DIVISION IMMEDIATELY ASSAULTED THE LEFT FLANK OF THE UNION LINE THAT WAS ATTACKING TOWARD SHARPSBURG.

THE UNIT ON THE EXTREME UNION LEFT THAT HILL ENGAGED WAS THE 16TH CONNECTICUT.

WHEEL **LEFT!** FORM UP!!

THE 16TH CONNECTICUT WAS BRAND NEW. THEY HAD ONLY BEEN ISSUED THEIR RIFLES TEN DAYS BEFORE.

THEY HAD RECEIVED NO WEAPONS TRAINING AT ALL.

HOW DO YOU LOAD THIS THING?

MANY DIED WITH THEIR RIFLES UNFIRED.

THE SURVIVORS BROKE AND RAN. FEW WOULD BLAME THEM.

THE 14TH RHODE ISLAND AND THE 8TH CONNECTICUT FLED THE FIELD AS WELL.

UNION COMMANDERS PANICKED. BURNSIDE ORDERED A RETREAT ALL THE WAY BACK TO ANTIETAM CREEK.

COLONEL KIMBALL, I ORDER YOU TO FALL BACK.

WITH DUE RESPECT, GENERAL WILLCOX, MY MEN GO OFF THIS FIELD UNDER MY ORDERS. THEY ARE NOT BEATEN!

UNION FORCES OUTNUMBERED THE CONFEDERATES BY MORE THAN TWO TO ONE, BUT BURNSIDE BELIEVED HE WAS BEATEN.

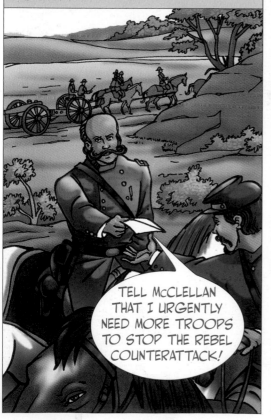

TELL McCLELLAN THAT I URGENTLY NEED MORE TROOPS TO STOP THE REBEL COUNTERATTACK!

McCLELLAN REFUSED. HE SAID HE HAD "NO MORE INFANTRY."

IN FACT HE HAD TWO WHOLE CORPS IN RESERVE. THE CONFEDERATES COULD HAVE BEEN TOTALLY DEFEATED IF THE UNION HAD MADE ONE MORE BIG PUSH.

BY SUNDOWN, THE BATTLE WAS OVER, AND 22,000 MEN LAY DEAD OR WOUNDED.

IT WAS THE SINGLE BLOODIEST DAY IN AMERICAN HISTORY.

ONE SOLDIER LATER WROTE, "YOU COULD WALK FROM ONE END OF THE CORNFIELD TO THE OTHER WITHOUT STEPPING ON THE GROUND."

MORE AMERICAN GENERALS WERE KILLED IN THAT ONE DAY THAN WERE KILLED IN ALL OF WORLD WAR II.

LEE'S ARMY HAD PERFORMED A MIRACLE SIMPLY BY SURVIVING AGAINST IMPOSSIBLE ODDS . . .

. . . BUT THE CONFEDERATE DRIVE INTO THE NORTH WAS OVER.

ON NOVEMBER 7, 1862, PRESIDENT LINCOLN ORDERED McCLELLAN TO TURN COMMAND OF THE ARMY OVER TO BURNSIDE.

BURNSIDE WOULD SOON BE REPLACED AS WELL. (TODAY HE IS REMEMBERED MOST FOR THE FACIAL HAIR NAMED AFTER HIM, SIDEBURNS.)

EDGAR KIMBALL WAS PROMOTED TO GENERAL BUT WAS SHOT DEAD BY ANOTHER GENERAL DURING A DISPUTE OVER A PASSWORD.

MANY YEARS AFTER THE WAR, JOHN GORDON AND FRANCIS BARLOW, WHO HAD OPPOSED EACH OTHER AT THE SUNKEN ROAD, MET BY CHANCE AT A DINNER PARTY . . .

. . . AND BECAME THE BEST OF FRIENDS.

THE END

At the end of the battle, over 23,000 soldiers—12,000 Union and 11,000 Confederate—were dead, dying, wounded, or missing. This was a quarter of each army. Among them were eighteen generals, nine from each side.

★ **Oliver Wendell Holmes, Sr.**

★ *Writer Oliver Wendell Holmes, Sr., went to the Antietam battlefield to look for his son, Oliver, Jr. Soldier Oliver, Jr., survived the war and became a U.S. Supreme Court judge.*

On September 18, Lee was on the defensive, in case McClellan would attack again. McClellan did not, and Lee's army slipped away across the river in the late afternoon. That left the Union army in possession of the battlefield, making Antietam a technical victory. That was enough for Lincoln to issue his Emancipation Proclamation five days later.

The proclamation made it clear that the Union was fighting the war for the freedom of all people. The ordinary people of Europe understood that, so no European nation interfered in America's conflict. The fate of the South was now in its own hands.

Photographer Mathew Brady came to the Antietam battlefield as Union soldiers were burying the dead. In October, Brady opened an exhibit in New York City called "The Dead of Antietam." It was the first time anyone had seen the horrors of war in photographs. At the time, war was still thought to be something romantic and glorious.

"Mr. Brady has done something to bring home to us the terrible reality and earnestness of war. If he has not brought bodies and laid them on our dooryard and along the streets, he has done something very like it," wrote the *New York Times*.

"Let him who wishes to know what war is look at this series of illustrations," wrote American poet Oliver Wendell Holmes, Sr.

President Lincoln was displeased by the way General McClellan conducted the battle and especially his failure to chase Lee's army. However, by calling Antietam a victory he could not immediately remove McClellan from command. Lincoln made a visit to McClellan's headquarters at Sharpsburg on October 1 to get him to advance. Then, from Washington, Lincoln ordered him to advance. McClellan made excuses and did nothing. Finally, Lincoln removed him from command on November 10, 1862, replacing him with General Burnside.

★ The Antietam battlefield saw more casualties in a single day than on any other day on American soil in history.

★ President Lincoln (left) was unhappy that McClellan (right) did not pursue the Confederates immediately. Lincoln relieved McClellan of command not long after the battle.

artillery Large, heavy guns that are mounted on wheels or tracks.

barrage A heavy outpouring of many things at once.

canister A round container.

column A formation in which soldiers are placed one behind the other.

dismal Causing, feeling, or showing gloom or depression.

disposal The act of throwing out or away.

diversionary Drawing attention away from the main concern.

divine Of, from, or like a god.

engage To take part or involve oneself.

infantry The branch of an army trained to fight on foot.

inflict To cause pain or suffering.

initial Of or happening at the beginning.

intact Not harmed or damaged.

musket A gun with a long barrel used before the invention of rifles.

muzzle The front of a gun barrel.

patent office A government agency that examines claims to inventions.

picket A soldier positioned to protect his main army from surprise attack.

proclamation A verbal or written public announcement.

regiment A unit of troops made up of two or more battalions.

round Ammunition for a single shot from a gun.

secede To formally withdraw from a group or organization, often to form another organization.

sect A group of people who share interests or beliefs.

skirmish A minor fight between small bodies of troops.

uplift To encourage.

vain Conceited.

volley A discharge of bullets from a gun.

volunteer A person who does a job freely and usually without pay.

★For More Information★

ORGANIZATIONS

Antietam National Battlefield Park
P.O. Box 158
Sharpsburg, MD 21782-0158
(301) 432-5124
Web site: www.nps.gov/anti

National Civil War Museum
P.O. Box 1861
Harrisburg, PA 17105-1861
(717) 260-1861

FOR FURTHER READING

Bolotin, Norman. *The Civil War A to Z*. New York: Dutton Children's Books, 2002.

Collier, Christopher. *Slavery and the Coming of the American Civil War, 1831–1861*. Salt Lake City, UT: Benchmark Books, 1999.

Hughes, Chris. *The Battle of Antietam*. Farmington Hills, MI: Blackbirch Press, 2001.

Ray, Delia. *A Nation Torn: The Story of How the Civil War Began*. New York: Puffin, 1996.

Sandler, Martin, W. *Civil War*. New York: HarperTrophy, 1991.

Stevens, Norman. *Antietam 1862: The Civil War's Bloodiest Day*. Oxford, England: Osprey Publishing, 1994.

★Index★

WEB SITES

Due to the changing nature of Internet links, the Rosen Publishing Group, Inc., has developed an online list of Web sites related to the subject of this book. This site is updated regularly. Please use this link to access the list:

http://www.rosenlinks.com/gbcw/ant